When the Righteous Cry Out

Renay K. Allen

Copyright © 2024 by Renay K. Allen

All rights reserved. No part of this book may be reproduced or transmitted in any form or by any means without written permission from the author.

ISBN- 979-889292006-3

Printed in USA by lulu publishing (https://www.lulu.com)

Unless otherwise stated, Scripture is taken from the King James Version, 1987. The KJV is public domain in the United States.

Names and segments of events were altered to protect the autonomy of individuals.

Cover: Designed using canva.com

Dedication

I would like to, first, dedicate this book to my Abba, Heavenly Father for answering my prayers. Oh, how I love Jesus, the one Who sacrificed His life so that I could receive eternal life.

To the Holy Spirit that quickened in my spirit to do what thus said the LORD.

And finally, to my parents, the late Turner Johnson, Jr., and the late Katie Mae Johnson. I love you.

Author's Note

Some of these stories go back more than 20 years. The people identified in the book by their first name and last initial are real people, but some of the names have been altered to respect their identity.

Acknowledgements

There are a number of wonderful people that I would like to acknowledge for encouraging me to follow the voice of God and make this project a priority.

Mr. Walter Lee Freeman, thank you so much for encouraging me to become a writer and author. You have been such an inspiration in this journey. You never stopped encouraging me to move forward for many years.

Dana La Voz, thank you for allowing GOD to use you by outlining this project for me. Sharing the vision that God wanted me to see regarding writing books and beyond. The time spent with you has been very rewarding and invaluable.

My Diamond Sisters from the Diamond Academy who all witnessed the Holy Spirit speak boldly and directly to me at the 2017 Prayer Summit at the Georgia Baptist Conference Center in Toccoa Georgia, asking me, "Why was I delaying the plan He had drawn out to me?" Thank you for praying for me to do the will of the Lord Jesus.

I would like to Thank Cherry English and Lillie Grace for helping me get started on writing this book.

I would like to Thank my Chancellor Constance Watson as well as my Diamond Sisters Michelle Murray and Bernadette Futrell for sharing how you got your books completed and assisted me where needed.

Thanks Lena Driskell-Holt, from God Ordain Works, for reminding me that it is a privilege to serve and the importance of being obedient to the Holy Spirit as well as, reminding me God uses His children to encourage others and to carve out time to write God's book.

I would like to send a HEARTY Thank you to Dr. Shonda Hill who asked to meet with me and saw my book and immediately got the process rolling with copywriting and getting the e-book out there until I am able to have it printed and published in book format. May God bless you abundantly for being my accountability partner, teacher, and helping me move forward with this vision God gave me.

I must thank my inspiring family for never doubting me when I shared with you what God had told me to do. I am so grateful to have such a loving family: Jermaine Allen Sr., Kraynewskia Onibode, Kaylah Allen, India Allen, Jermaine Allen, Jr. Katelin Allen, Kristine Allen, Judah Allen, and my two granddaughters, Nikeria Allen, and Zoe-Ayomi Onibode. My family and church family Thank you all so much!

I must thank the editors and every person whom I asked to share your testimony with me for the book and to everyone who actually sent their testimonies in! To the late Pastor Emill Bridges—who met me once in person in 2017— and who sent me a message via Facebook messenger out of the blue stating, "whatever it is God says it is time to finish and release it to the body, do it!" And followed up by asking, "Have you written any books?"

The answer to your question Pastor Bridges is, "Yes!"

I pray the testimonies bless you and the body of Christ!

Contents

Introduction 1

Chapter 1 - God is My Banner of Protection 7

Chapter 2 - God Can Deliver and Restore You! 11

Chapter 3 - God is My Healer 15

Chapter 4 - God Can Make the Lame Walk Again 23

Chapter 5 - God is an Encourager 29

Chapter 6 - Jehovah-Jireh My Provider 33

Chapter 7 - God Can Lift Your Spirit 35

Chapter 8 - Seeking God for Clarity 37

Chapter 9 - God Can Beat Cancer 41

Chapter 10 - Can God Still Heal the Blind? 43

Chapter 11 - Hope for the Hopeless 47

Chapter 12 - Can God Still Raise the Dead? 53

Chapter 13 - When God Knows Your Need 57

Chapter 14 - God is Still Performing Miracles 59

Chapter 15 - Nobody but God 63

Chapter 16 - Prayer is a Sustainer 69

Chapter 17 - I Had to Take this Time to Give this Testimony 71

Chapter 18 - God Heals Little Children 73

Chapter 19 - God Can Restore 75

Chapter 20 - If He Did It for Her, He Will Do It for Me 79

Chapter 21 - When You Receive Bad News Unexpectedly .. 83

Chapter 22 - God is Dependable 87

Chapter 23 - Only By Faith 91

Chapter 24 - Wait on the Lord 95

Introduction

People should not have to wait until Sunday to hear powerful testimonies!
This is where this work began.

In 2018, I walked into my closet praising God for a testimony that had taken place in my life and said to myself, "I sure hate that people have to wait until Sunday to hear testimonies." That is when a clear voice said, "You will write a book about testimonies."

I began praising and thanking God! Hallelujah!

This book has been put on pause many times due to me feeling like I could not handle the assignment given. I literally went back to college after 20 years to complete my Bachelor of Science degree in Business Management for God to show me that I can do all things through Him. This book was to be written prior to the Coronavirus Pandemic so that people all over the world would have a renewed sense of hope while being placed in a stay-at-home predicament that looked hopeless to many.

Even though I did not follow the plan perfectly, I serve a God of second chances and have secured the testimonies of many that I know will encourage you in the days ahead. Life is a struggle. This journey is not easy. But all things are possible through Christ Jesus.

God has allowed me to pray for so many people. I have seen so many miracles manifested only through Christ Jesus. Perhaps if you are struggling today, one of these testimonies will give you the strength to "keep on keeping on" or to fight the good fight of faith.

As I was getting dressed back on August 1, 2018, at 5:30 AM, the Holy Spirit simply whispered, what else would I have you write about? It's truly the blood of the Lamb and the testimonies of God's people that helps them overcome. He said, "He is in the SAVING business." Wow! is all I could say. Isaiah 12:2 (KJV) was the verse I opened the Bible to that states, "Behold, God is my salvation, I will trust, and not be afraid: for the Lord Jehovah is my strength and my song; He also is my salvation." Glory Hallelujah. Revelation 12:11 (KJV) states. "And they overcame him by the blood of the Lamb, and by the word of their testimony; and they loved not their lives unto death."

On July 4, 2018, the hymn and words to the song, "There is Power in the Blood, "composed by Lewis E. Jones (1845 -1936) began to ring in my mind and heart. Here are the words to the hymn.

Chorus:
There is power, power, wonder working power in the blood of the Lamb.

There is power, power, wonder working power in the blood of the Lamb.

Verse 1:
Would you be free from the burden of sin? There's power in the blood, power in the blood; Would you over evil a victory win? There is wonderful power in the blood.

Verse 2:
Would you be free from your passion and pride? There is power in the blood, power in the blood; Come for a cleansing to Cal-va-ry's tide; There's wonderful power in the blood.

Verse 3:
Would you be whiter, much whiter than snow?
There's power in the blood, power in the blood, power in the blood; Sin stains have lost in its life giving flow; There's wonderful power in the blood.

Verse 4 (final verse)
Would you do service for Jesus your King?
There's power in the blood, power in the blood; Would you live daily His praises to sing?
There's wonderful power in the blood.

As the Holy Spirit would have me awake and place the song in heart, I began to sing the chorus to the song and then, He had me grab the Hymnal off my nightstand and turn to the words and review the verses. Now I have sung the verses on many occasions, especially during Communion on first Sunday services. But today! I really took a deeper look at each word in each verse and realized God is still asking those questions today. Would you be free from the burden of sin?

Would you over evil a victory win?
Would you be free from your passion and pride?
Would you be whiter, much whiter than snow?
Would you do service for Jesus your King?
Would you live daily His praises to sing?

So I'll ask, "Will your answer be, yes?"

During the 2016, 2017 year, I was asked to write a devotional for our Women's Group. As I wrote, I was praying Dear LORD God, help me to write one that would give you all of the Glory. He pressed upon my heart to write about my encounter with Him where everything in my life changed. I was assigned Prayer Warrior over my church during that time. The church was Beulah Cathedral led by the late Bishop Victor P. Smith in 2000. At that time I was excited for the opportunity and twenty-four years later I am still excited for that opportunity. During that time, I was going in and out of tribulations—fiery trials I should say— but I remained focused. In 2009, I lost my job and began going through what appeared as a fiery trial that continued in a downward spiral. I was losing properties and my credit was at an all-time low. I could not gain employment so my finances were in shambles. I could not regain or reincorporate. It felt like I was stuck in a hole and would be doomed forever. I had seven children and I was a caregiver to my mother who was ailing in health. I was invited to a prayer breakfast by the women at one of our sister churches. You had to be there on-time by 8:00 am on that Saturday morning. I was pressing my way there and arrived early. I sat in the car for a little while and meditated, then I went in about 10 minutes early. I did not want to be late. As I waited for others to arrive and the prayer breakfast to begin, I noticed it was very quiet. There were even signs that stated, "Shhh...be quiet before the LORD." As the room filled with women, the facilitator got up at exactly 8:01 AM and locked the door. This was strange as this was not part of past practices. She came to the front center of the room and stated, "The LORD instructed me to lock the door, I am not allowed to let anyone in at this point." She then stated, "look around...GOD has said this is the way Heaven is going to be. The ones you thought would be here may not necessarily be here and the ones you may have thought wouldn't be here are here." This is how it is going to be on the Day of the LORD. Wow, is all I could think to myself. Then the facilitator stated, "God wants to bless each of you here today and He wants you to ask Him for what you want." I became excited because I really needed a huge financial breakthrough. As I shared, I was losing everything I owned. I, then remembered Solomon's prayer to the LORD at the age of 8 years old. His prayer was not a worldly or selfish prayer. It was how he could be a blessing to the LORD and God's people. As I pondered what he asked God, I wondered how I, too, could ask for something that benefited my family alone despite how many of God's people were going through worse situations than I. That is when I asked God to please help me pray for others and see Him move so that I could praise Him. The Lord answered my prayer. I have seen Him move in so many ways and I want to share some of these testimonies with you. Be blessed!

Chapter 1

God is My Banner of Protection

By: Renay Allen

In October 2017, I went through a serious test regarding my eldest son, Jermaine who had a life-threatening injury from playing football.

When I picked him up from his game, he took a long time to come out, which was unusual. He was walking strangely and was in excruciating pain. I pleaded with him to let me take him to the hospital. He refused. On the way home, he asked if he could use the car and I told him no because he was hurting. This was the first time I said, "no" and I meant it. He said he wanted to get food and told him I would take him. We went home and he grabbed his wallet while I waited in the car. While walking in the house, I noticed he was still walking strangely. After grabbing our order from a local restaurant, returning home, and sitting down to eat, he began eating slowly, which was not the norm for him. I asked him to please take some medicine, shower and go right to bed. He went upstairs, he turned on the shower and was undressing when I heard him call for me. He afterwards collapsed and could not move. I was in shock.

Instead of calling 911 first, I immediately called his coach and asked "what happened to my son?" The coach was confused and said that he appeared fine at the game. I informed the coach that my son had collapsed and that I could not pick him up. Not receiving any help from the coach regarding the cause of my son's collapse, I then remembered to call 911. I then begged my son to try crawling down the steps. Unfortunately, he could not move and was in extreme pain. I told the 911 operator his situation and they asked if he had vomited. I said no — at least not while I was speaking with them. They asked a few more questions, gave instructions that my son followed, and afterwards ended the call. My son looked at me and said, "Mom, I believe I am dying." After hearing these words, I ran into my room, anointed myself, and prayed fervently. I called a prayer partner to pray with me. She could hear my son saying that he was dying. She asked what hospital I was taking him to and I told her Hillendale. She called our Pastor and agreed to meet us there. The EMT sent a non-emergency ambulance despite me saying that the situation was an emergency. They sent two gaunt paramedics who could not pick up my son. The paramedics told him he would have to get up and walk. This was not possible. By this time, I had called my other children who had come over to help me get my son onto a gurney and down the stairs. We finally got him into the ambulance. I drove my vehicle behind them. The hospital was told that this was a serious emergency and that my son needed immediate medical help. The hospital staff took him off the gurney and put him in a wheelchair and rolled him into the waiting room! He was hurting so badly. I felt helpless and kept thinking of how he had turned 18 years old just three days ago. The people at the front desk who checked him in were vulgar and kept saying that since he was 18, he could talk for himself. They soon found out the extend of the emergency when he tried to stand and immediately fell to the floor. He was hurting so badly, but the hospital refused to offer any assistance. I asked if they could call another ambulance to take him to another hospital that could help him. They said "no" and that they would charge a fee for transferring him to another hospital since they had already checked him in. My church family arrived and we prayed for my son and prayed for a couple more patients waiting to be seen. In addition to my son, there was also another teammate that had a concussion who had been waiting two hours. This was a sign that my son would be waiting a long time–time that we did not have. An experienced church member in the waiting room with us accessed my son's weight and height, and determined that he had approximately 45 minutes to get him immediate help, otherwise he was not going to make it. He ran to get his vehicle and picked up my son and put him in a wheelchair and rolled him to his SUV. He transported him to a nearby hospital where they were waiting to receive him. We explained the mis-treatment at the first hospital and my son's dire need for medical attention. How the first facility was literally willing to let my son die in the waiting room. The staff immediately began working with him. They did an MRI and other body scans and determined he had a ruptured kidney and was bleeding inside. They said he would have to be air-flighted to Grady Hospital or Atlanta Medical Hospital. I called my husband because the helicopter was already on the way. My husband said, "have them take him to Grady Hospital," as they had the number one trauma unit. They had a team of surgeons waiting to see him upon arrival. My son was heavily sedated because of the extent of his injury. He continued to be in excruciating pain. To make matters worse, the staff was in conflict. The lead doctor was in favor of removing the ruptured kidney. However, another team of doctors stopped her and said "no," they were performing the surgery to save the kidney because of his age. They feared that if he was ever in another emergency accident and lost the last kidney, he would be without a kidney and that would be detrimental. I was in favor of not having the kidney removed and appreciated that the team overrode the head doctor's decision. We prayed with the doctors and declared my son's healing. It was a process. For days, I would spend the night at the hospital and then go to work the following morning. I had a team of care-givers to include my spouse, coaches, family members and church members who would stay with my son after he got out of the intensive care unit. His teammates would visit as well. I am excited to report that my son was saved and healed by the power of the Holy Spirit, prayer, and the Blood of the Lamb. To God be all the glory! My son was left with two kidneys.

Chapter 2
God Can Deliver and Restore You!
As told by Minister Ellis

My testimony is both familiar and unique. I was a drug addict, alcoholic, cigarette- smoking sinner on my way to hell. I was wallowing in sin for approximately 15 years with no hope, no purpose, and no future. I had no real relationship with our Lord and Savior Jesus Christ. My mother raised me in church. I knew better than I was acting and had no excuse. I was simply lost. The enemy trapped me in the early stages of my adult life —at a time when I thought I knew it all and that no one could tell me anything. I am so grateful to God, because even in my sin, stupidity, and stubbornness, God was still watching over me. I repeat, I was headed straight to hell, but God looked at me and saw that I was a willing vessel, an unfinished work, and a broken pot. Early one Sunday morning, I was sitting in a park in the middle of downtown Atlanta, Ga., after a weekend of frivolous, reckless, and debaucherously living. I was down and out, down-trodden, and dejected. Simply put, I was at the end of my road. Things we're looking pretty bad for me. I was at the lowest point of my life. Then God sent a man to minister to me. He invited me to church. I accepted his invitation. I will never forget that day. I told him I was hungry. He said no problem, that he would get me something to eat after church. I went to church with him. I had a wonderful time in the Lord. Everyone accepted me at the church with open arms. I truly loved the church and the feeling of being accepted. I really wanted to change my life. God gave me an avenue! I started attending the church on a regular basis. Before long, the church—along with the Bishop, the Pastor and other leaders at the church allowed me and seven other men to live at the church until we got a job, and got on our feet enough to get our own place of residence. I thank God for the church and its caring members, despite opposition from the enemy. I stopped getting high, drinking and smoking cigarettes. Most of all I developed a closer relationship with God and the church. I attended Sunday school and Bible study on a regular basis. Over a very short period of time, I won Bible study quiz contests. I received perfect attendance for Sunday school. I was an usher for a short period of time. I knew I was in the right church. There was one nice lady who accepted me into her home and into her family. Without her support and encouragement, even now, I don't believe I would be where I am today spiritually.

One evening, after Bible study I met and befriended the late Bishop Victor P. Smith. We started traveling to Florida every two weeks to further and maintain the functioning of churches in Jacksonville and Apopka. After 2 years, I informed the Bishop that God called me to preach. Again, after much opposition from the enemy, I was allowed to preach my trial sermon in October of 1999. I continued to go to Florida with the Bishop until I moved back to California in 2001. I was the guest speaker at our youth conference in Gulfport MS, in 2000, where I shared my testimony to 300 youth and young adults. I have been an active member in COCHUSA since I joined the church and gave my life to the Lord in 1998. I have been saved, sanctified, filled with the Holy spirit, and delivered from all the traps and snares of the devil for 21 years. And I can't thank God enough for the opportunity he has given me to teach and preach his word. As I have attended Bible school and taken numerous Bible courses. I have studied under some great men of God, great pastors, and the wonderful Bishop Smith. I thank Missionary Sister Renay Allen, for opening up her heart and her home to me and praying with and for me. I still remember having Bible study at her home. Her obedience to the Lord has changed my life and the life of my family for generations to come.

Chapter 3

God is My Healer

As told by Elder and Sister Terrell

The below is the testimony of Eld. and Sis. Terrell regarding how God healed her.
(Spoken in Eld. Terrell's own words)

On 10/9/2018, I texted,
Good morning, Missionary Allen.
I'm in the hospital due to blockages in my heart. Please keep me lifted in prayer today. I am going in at about 1pm so it will be late this afternoon before I can give a report on the status of my health. Thank you for your prayers.

Elder Nash texted me and he also needs prayer. He said that his doctor put him in the hospital this morning. I don't know which hospital yet, but he needs a miracle right now. Thank you so much. God's healing grace is sufficient for this day for both of us. I came through the catheterization fine. They did find some blockages and so I will be here until we execute a plan. Thank you again for the prayers and I will keep you informed as we progress. God bless.

As I am writing this, Sis. Burkhalter spoke to Sis Nash. Elder Nash will go home tomorrow, and Sis. Nash's cast will come off. Look at God, Won't He Do It! She is so happy, and thank you for the prayers.

10/10/18
I really appreciate your faithfulness and prayers. May His richest blessings be yours!
This is Sister Betty Rhyme's message to you.

Judges 6:2 says...... And the angel of the Lord appeared to Gideon and said, "The Lord is with thee, thou mighty man of Valor"!!!!!
Praise the Lord! We believe Your Word oh God. I will REJOICE IN THE LORD ALWAYS, and again I WILL REJOICE. Ain't nobody mad but the enemy. Let's Celebrate JESUS!

10/11/18
My room number is 316. Although this room number will change, it reminds me of the scripture John 3:16.

10/12/18
Missionary Allen, with the help of God and through your prayers my body, spirit, and soul is being healed, sustained, and restored. May God bless you and your ministry as you labor in His vineyard. Never take what you do lightly for He has heard and continues to hear your prayers! Thank you so much!

Sis. Terrell shared the below.

George was moved from the ICU today. They are working to control the pain. He is drowsy and somewhat alert. The nurse did not say he could not have visitors but did say he did not need to get excited or laugh much. Any visits should be brief. We'll see what tomorrow brings. Thank you for your prayers & love. We praise God for His goodness & thank you for your prayers.

10/13/18
Sis. Terrell updated…

I WILL CONTINUE TO KEEP YOU INFORMED OF GEORGE'S PROGRESS.

George was moved from the ICU yesterday. His pain is better. It is most obvious when he coughs or moves. But, movement and exercise is necessary. The goal for today is to walk at least three times and to blow into the "device" more consistently. This will help his lungs and prevent pneumonia. Visits should continue to be brief. He still should not get excited or laugh too much. Thank you for your prayers & love. We praise God for His goodness.

10/14/18
Sis. Terrell exclaimed…

Good evening, George is getting closer to going home!! All cords and tubes are to be removed today. His drains have also been removed. He's being weaned from oxygen. He is coughing up what is required. Coughing & walking still leaves him winded & he continues to experience some pain.

We continue praising God, for His goodness. We are thankful for your prayers, love & support.

10/15/18
Sis. Terrell joyously messages...

We are headed home!! Praise GOD!!

10/17/19
Hereby perceive we the love of God, because he laid down his life for us: and we ought to lay down our lives for the brethren.
1 John 3:16 KJV
https://bible.com/bible/1/1jn.3.16.KJV

10/19/18
Thank you so much. The prayers of the righteous avail much. God has heard and continues to hear you. God bless.

10/25/19
Thank you so much. The prayers are working. Unfortunately, the only time we really know that God is near is when He does something that nobody else can do. He's been with me, thanks to the prayers of the saints and faithful believers like you and your army of praying women. I thank God for each of you!

10/30/18

Sis. Terrell updates….

Good morning. They are trying to tell me that I have the flu. Getting ready to go to urgent care to be tested. Will text you later this afternoon. Be blessed.

I respond…

Okay thanks for the update. Binding up the flu and anything else coming against you in the matchless name of Jesus.

Sis. Terrell reports…

No flu, lungs clear. God is a great BIG God! Hallelujah!

11/13/18

Bro. Terrell reports…

Thank you so much. Getting ready to go see the surgeon for the first time since the operation this morning. Pray that God will give them wisdom and patience to carefully examine my body to know that all is well. Everyone seems so focused on their specialty that they do not examine the whole being.

May God richly bless you in your labor of love and prayer!

I respond…

I most certainly am praying for your request right now.

Bro. Terrell updates…

Thank you. Just left the surgeon's office and he has released me. Praise God! Your prayers have power. Blessed!

Glory Hallelujah!! Our GOD is so mighty!!!

11/6/18
I encourage Eld. Terrell….

Hi Elder the Righteous are crying out to God for your healing. We are trusting only Him to do what only He can.
Just know that the Lord hears the cries of the righteous! I had a fever all last week, no flu, and no reason for the fever. My blood pressure went up Saturday morning and I was concerned about a stroke. They looked all weekend. There was no reason, but they fed me with at least 3 different classes of antibiotics. Nothing was growing on the cultures taken. Then Monday afternoon, an attendant came in and looked at my left lung and said that there was fluid in the lining of my lungs. She put a needle in my back and pulled about a liter of fluid out of my lung.! Praise God! What a mighty God we serve. She told me that she had seen the fluid on the CT scan that I had completed on Saturday. No one else had seen it, I guess. Came home last night and I voted today. What a mighty God we serve!

11/9/18
I stated….
Elder please know that I am praying for you!
He responded:
I know that you are praying, and I really appreciate you and all that you do. I will be there tomorrow. Just pray that I have enough strength to make it through the services. God bless!

11/22/18
Eld. Terrell happily updates…

Happy thanksgiving to you and your family. You have helped me to see this day and experience the healing virtue of our God.
I pray that the Lord bless you my Sister and supply all of your needs according to His riches in glory by Christ Jesus. The Lord knows your transportation needs. I am asking Jesus to supply your needs for His name's sake and we will praise His glorious name!

I replied…
To God be the glory!! Hallelujah. What a Thanksgiving! I will receive those blessings.

12/17/18
Eld. Terrell gives a faith-filled update…

Good evening, Missionary Allen,
God bless your faithfulness to your calling. I'm gaining some feeling back from nerve damage, which is good. I went to a pulmonary doctor who said my lungs are in great condition. I just need my rib cage to finish healing. God is very good! He hears your prayers and they are working on my behalf. Thank you so much!

Glory Hallelujah!!!

Chapter 4
God Can Make the Lame Walk Again
As told by Arthur J.

I met Brother Arthur at a National Convention in the summer of 2017 in Durham, North Carolina. I went to a healing service and the Bishop who was facilitating the service called for Brother Arthur to come forward. An assistant rolled Bro. Arthur to the front of the church. The Bishop began speaking directly to him that he would be healed. He then asked some brothers at the service to help Brother Arthur out of the wheelchair.

It seemed surreal.

Bro. Arthur's legs were so small and frail. They looked like pegs. At first, Bro. Arthur only took a step or two at that service. The Bishop continued to encourage him to walk. However, Bro. Arthur did not appear to be receptive. The Bishop was sure that he could walk, but Bro. Arthur needed encouragement. The Bishop called me over and asked me to share my mother's testimony from when the Bishop had a healing service at my church earlier in the Spring. I began sharing how God moved in my mother's body when she had been diagnosed with breast cancer. I continued on how the LORD God had moved miraculously in her body. It confused the doctors so much that they asked my mom to get dressed and to not come back again! The hospital workers said that somebody really loved her and informed her to keep doing what she was doing. [My mother's testimony is further down in this book]. As I continued to testify, my son began having a migraine. He never had a migraine before. However, the Bishop would not allow me to stop witnessing. He stated it was an attack and that the enemy did not want me to share with Brother Arthur. I began praying for his complete healing. I did not know the history behind what happened to him. I just knew that he was bound by a wheelchair when I last saw him at the convention.

The below is the story behind Bro. Arthur's powerful testimony in his own words...

I am a survivor of eight gunshots. It was late one night on September 1, 2011. I was in a two-way robbery in Westland, MI. Everything was my fault. I felt that I had no other choice but to rob someone. The robbery was for a quarter pound of weed. I was with 3 other gentlemen who were determined to go through with the plan. I was convinced that we should leave, however, my friend got out of the car anyway. At that point I had no other choice but to get out. None of us had the cash for the weed purchase ($1400 for 4oz), and I was the only one with the gun. It was two of them and three of us. One of the guys had on a Gucci backpack and did all the talking. His words were "Y'all niggas got that cash?" From the tone of his voice, I knew what his intentions were. I insisted that he show me the product before I showed him the cash— although I didn't have it. We kept going back and forth until eventually I pulled my gun out first. My friend slowly began backing up towards the car as I was going through with the robbery. The friend of the guy I was robbing took his gun out while standing behind me on one side. As I took the bag with the drugs in it and was turning around to head back to the car, that's when my friend yelled at the top of his lungs "Sugg! watch out." Seconds later, gunshots started ringing. I was shot twice and started running to get some distance in between us. I took about 5 steps before one of the bullets struck my spine. I never knew how many times I was shot, nor where I specifically was shot on my body. The only bullet that I legitimately felt was the one that paralyzed me. Once going down I stayed lying face flat until the gun shots eventually came to an end, and the footsteps around me started to fade away. I flipped over onto my back to sit and looked at my legs in disbelief. I had been paralyzed.

It hurt to sit in that position because I was unaware that I had been shot 6 times in the buttocks (2 times in the left cheek, 4 times in the right.) As I flipped back over into the position I was originally in (face down) the guy with the Gucci bag whom I shot at, came creeping around the bushes, running back towards me. I just knew he was coming back to finish me off because he saw that I was still alive. At that moment, I called upon God. His response was "be still."

The gun that I had was on my right-hand side, and the Gucci bag with the drugs was on my left hand side. He ran up to me and grabbed my gun and walked around onto my left-hand side to grab the bag that I robbed from him. At this point, the guy is standing over me. I just knew he was going to kill me, yet all he did was grab the bag with the drugs in it and left. For years I was puzzled as to why he didn't kill me. Any real killer would have taken the bag and also killed me in retaliation for trying to kill him first. I was left for dead by both my friends and the guy I was trying to rob.

I laid helpless with no assistance for almost forty-five minutes. I couldn't move and felt myself getting weaker and weaker. Suddenly, out of nowhere, an ambulance arrived with a police officer. They rushed me to the hospital and I immediately went into surgery. My body began to go into shock on the way to the hospital. "Am I going to make it?" I said to the paramedics, asking them to be honest with me. His response was "honestly, it isn't looking too good but we're going to do the best we can." Two days later I woke up from a coma to my family crying and my brother GOING CRAZZYYYYY. It was the first time anyone other than my parents, my aunt, and pastor was allowed to visit me. I remained in the hospital for over a month where I started my journey of Physical Therapy. Once being released from the hospital, I began out-patient visits until my insurance stopped paying for my sessions. I continued working-out on my own. I went from a wheelchair to a walker. A walker to two canes. From two canes to the natural strength and stability God had given me again to walk on my own. Through the power of God and the prayers of the saints, three and a half years later, I was walking without any assistance! Praise the Lord!

Chapter 5
God is an Encourager
By: Renay Allen

How many of you know that God hears your thoughts from afar? I am a witness to this fact. After about 30 years of being out of school, I decided to return to complete my bachelor's degree in business management. I was 49 years old at the time and had a son who needed to get his undergraduate education. In addition, I was encouraging my daughter, who received her master's degree about 7 years prior to get her Doctorate degree. She said, "Mom, if you get your master's degree I will go back to get my doctorate." I agreed. I was unemployed and my children were going to school virtually due to COVID-19. I felt that it was a great time to meet the challenge. I, therefore, enrolled in Colorado State University-Global Campus after researching several schools. They offered accelerated courses, so I was excited to finish sooner rather than later. However, I did not realize how challenging and rigorous the courses would be given that 18 weeks of studies would be covered in 9 weeks.

While writing a paper on the topic entitled, "Am I getting to the age where employers are overlooking me for employment?" I received a call for a job offer. I completed the interview and they asked me to start in two days. They wanted me to complete the paperwork the next day. I was flabbergasted! It seemed as if the employer had read my paper. It was 100% God. He knew my thoughts. I completed my degree at 50 years old and graduated Summa Cum Laude. My other honors included, the Gold Key International Honor Society, the National Society of Leaders, and the Honor Society —all while working full-time, home schooling three children, being a wife and an active board member in several organizations. This was only possible through Christ. As soon as this book is complete, I plan to go back to school to get my master's degree to further challenge my daughter and become more marketable. I firmly believe that if you have a true desire to improve and do other things, God will hear you and will direct you if you will step out on faith.

The task of finishing my degree was not easy. I spent many nights praying, staying up studying, and sacrificing leisure weekend time—as most of that time was dedicated to completing my assignments. My family could not believe the amount of work I had to complete and how rigorous the assignments were. There is no way I could have done this without the help of God. My community of friends and family were impressed. My mentor even admitted that said could only take courses part-time. Others were simply amazed that I was able to stay the course. It was only possible with prayer and trusting God to see me through. If He did it for me, He will do the same for you!

Chapter 6
Jehovah-Jireh My Provider
By: Renay Allen

In June of 2021, I received a call to pick up a car. The only stipulation was that I needed to get there as soon as possible because the family with the vehicle was relocating to North Carolina. They owned three vehicles, but only wanted to take two on their travel. The vehicle was in mint condition and was a top-of-the line Buick product. The prayer team had been praying with me for God to provide my children with cars. Having this additional vehicle would afford me the opportunity to provide one of the children with my current car.

But God knows the end from the beginning. He knew about three weeks, after providing me with that vehicle, that the current car would be hit by a reckless driver and would total that vehicle. The person hit my 17-year old daughter, ran her into a pole, and never stopped to see if she was okay. This same driver almost hit another driver. A lady pulled over to check to see if my daughter was okay. When she did not see anyone moving in the car, the lady ran to rescue my daughter. My daughter turned out to be fine. To God be the glory!

God makes plans ahead of time to keep us even when we are unaware of what is going to happen. You have heard the Saints say "God keeps us from dangers seen and unseen." He continued to provide so that my family could take my daughter for check-ups and manage appointments for everyone else in the household.

There was not a delay. God ensured my daughter's safety. I want to encourage someone who is in need of a vehicle today to pray for God to send you a breakthrough. I have had a total of five cars gifted to me. As soon as the enemy destroyed one vehicle the Lord immediately replenished and supplied me with a replacement. You must trust God to do just what He said He would do. He said He will provide all of your needs according to his riches in glory by Christ Jesus. He is faithful and blesses His people. I have to give Him all of the praise, glory and honor for being my Jehovah-Jireh. Thank you Jesus, MY PROVIDER!

~Renay

Chapter 7
God Can Lift Your Spirit
By: Tony B.

During a very difficult time, God allowed me to pray for a brother in need named Tony B. He was going through a divorce. His finances, nor his credit, were where he wanted them to be. Nevertheless, he was trying to get both in order.

This is Tony B's testimony...

I can testify that sometimes when life whips on you, there are prayer warriors you can talk to. While I was going through a valley of darkness Renay Allen kept me in prayer. I had recently gone through a divorce and was down in my spirit. I was renting from Renay's mom. She offered to sell me the house at a reasonable price. The house was older & needed some work, no one would finance it for me. This young woman of God would just call to check on me and lift me up in prayer on a regular basis. I could feel the spirit moving as other people were coming by to look at the house. Renay kept saying "IT'S GOD'S WILL TO NOT LET YOU GET THIS HOUSE BECAUSE HE HAS SOMETHING BETTER STORED UP FOR YOU!" Just like she said, I was approved for a brand-new home within 30 days. I was told I could have the home by Christmas of 2018. God looked past my low credit scores and blessed me despite all the obstacles. I had recently retired from my job, and recently divorced with one-income.

I Thank God for my blessing. I Thank God for Renay and for her prayers.

God showed up out of nowhere and provided me with the keys to a brand new home. This was truly a miracle that only God could provide.

Chapter 8
Seeking God for Clarity
By: *Cherry E.*

I first met my dear friend Renay Allen at a birthday celebration in the summer of 2017. Instantly we connected in the Spirit, for I sensed she was a woman who had this inner glow and tranquility about her. After talking and getting to know her a bit, I knew the peace I saw upon her countenance could only have come from God! I felt an immediate freedom to share with her details about my current relationship with someone whom I was dating—who now happens to be my fiancé—glory to God!

At that time, I didn't know if we, as a couple, should proceed towards getting married or not. For I was a "scared rabbit" so to speak! Even though I felt I was in love, I was reluctant to do the "marriage thing" again. The thought of taking on that journey again gave me the jitters!!

Renay gave me some Holy Spirit-filled advice. She said, "God already knows about your concerns." She encouraged me to pray and to allow God to help me. She continued, "allow God, foremost, to give you His peace and don't be anxious about anything. Let God help you with your own heart, and, as he promised, He will direct your path. You just need to acknowledge and allow Him to be right there in the midst of your situation regarding this relationship. Allow your man the opportunity to show you if he's truly the Godly man you asked God for. He, himself will surely prove whether he is or isn't the one God has for you. Just 'stand still and see the salvation of the Lord' and allow and enjoy the 'process of dating.'

She further stated, "Don't be in a hurry! Time and process go hand-in- hand when dating and getting to know each other is critical." I listened and received those wonderful, God-given words of wisdom. I'm so at peace in my relationship, and so thankful for the continued love and respect I'm receiving from my friend. This is truly the way God intended for a man to love a woman — desiring in a Godly way for him to want her for his wife. And thanks to God He has shown me that this man is my God-sent friend and "Boaz!" In September, 2018 we became engaged—yes, beautiful ring and all!! We married in 2019! I'm so thankful to my Spirit filled friend, Renay Allen for allowing the Holy Spirit to boldly speak through her on that summer day, giving her those words of encouragement to share with me. As she stated, "God is our friend and is concerned about us. Our Heavenly Father wants to be involved and glorified in every aspect of our lives, for His Name sake!"

A note from Renay…

Given that this book is published in 2024, I wanted to share that the marriage took place as planned and God is blessing their union. To God be the glory for hearing and answering the prayers of the righteous one. She sold her home, and relocated from Georgia back to her hometown in Philadelphia and they are as HAPPY as can be as a married couple.

Chapter 9

God Can Beat Cancer

By: Renay Allen

In 2008, my mother received the report that she had breast cancer. She was referred to several doctors, including one who performs mastectomies. She was told that they could remove all of the cancer, however, she was then told that, as a result, she would not be allowed to lift more than 5 lbs. during the recovery period. My mother asked, "Did you say that I can't lift more than 5 pounds?" She immediately got off the table, asked for her clothing, and said she was ready to go— there would be no surgery. My mother made this decision because at the time, both my sister and I were expecting. She wanted to hold her grandbabies and nothing was going to stand in her way.

Not even cancer.

The doctor explained that she had lobular cancer. This cancer type meant that it would reach out to other parts of her body. We prayed for God to move. We did not go back to any doctors.

At the time, my mother was 76 years of age. The following week after our visit to the doctor, we had a revival and my mother rededicated her life to Christ. We no longer spoke of her condition. Her decision to not receive treatment was one we all respected.

In 2011, my church was having a healing service. I told my mother that I wanted to go, and she said she wanted to go also. We both said that if people were being "slain in the spirit" we would not go to the altar. The Bishop that preached that service shared the account of Naaman in the Bible found in II Kings. After preaching, he took his anointing oil to the altar and asked who wanted to be healed? After noticing that the first people on whom the Bishop laid hands were still standing, we immediately went up to the altar to receive healing.

Sometime later, my mother went to the doctor for her annual check-up. They performed a breast image on her because I informed her doctor that she had not had an exam since her diagnosis. When my sister took her back for her results, the doctor that was sharing her results kept saying, "somebody really loves you!" over and over again. He began sharing her results with her and said, "Ma'am, since you had your last imaging done in 2008, absolutely nothing has changed, HALLELUJAH! It looks exactly the same." He asked that she get dressed and not come back again. He told her to keep doing what she was doing because the doctors could not explain how this could be. She was cancer free! She lived to the ripe age of 83 and did not pass with cancer. BUT GOD!

Chapter 10
Can God Still Heal the Blind?
By: Renay Allen

If asked the question, "Can God still heal the blind?" I would respond with a resounding "Yes!" Why? Because I know without a doubt that He is the same God yesterday, today, and forevermore. However, in addition to this truth being written in the Bible, I also personally witnessed it with my very own eyes.

Betty is a dear sister at my church. The retina in Betty's eye detached, causing her blindness.
Although she had surgery, it was unsuccessful. Her sight did not return to that eye as expected. Infection set up and she had a repeat episode of her retina detaching once again.

At this time in her life, she really began going through some fiery trials. But God!

The women's group of which she and I were a part, had been focusing on the topic, "Wilt Thou Be Made Whole?" God had me reading in the Bible where He personally healed the blind man through Christ Jesus. He made mud and placed it on the man's eyes.

When Jesus asked the blind man "what do you see?" The man replied, "I see people looking like trees." How did the man know what a tree looked like if he had been blind from birth? Only God!

Then Jesus repeated the process. The second time the man saw clearly. It was not that Jesus could not have completely healed him the first time. This is what happened with that sister. She was out of work, but she needed to work to generate income in order to pay for the first unsuccessful surgery. She was a bus driver and needed to see in order to drive the bus. She was torn. I shared with her what God had shared with me through the reading of His Word. I asked her if she would be made whole? She stated, "yes." We began praying and praying. She was anointed by the man of God according to the Word.

She afterwards, selected another eye professional since she was very displeased with her first surgeon. The current doctor could not believe how the first surgeon performed the procedure. He explained that he would have to redo the surgery. This was not what she desired. She was very nervous about the situation and, in addition, would now have to come up with the funds to have the surgery redone.

One day, as I was talking to this sister on the phone, my baby son, who was three years old, was playing with his toys. He suddenly stopped and walked over and told me to tell the person on the phone that her doctors and husband could only comfort her. But that If she was to be healed, God would do the healing. He returned to playing with his toys. She asked, "What did that baby just say?" I repeated his words and we began to cry out and thank God. I shared how God had revealed that the blind man that Jesus healed had to undergo a second procedure to see clearly again. We continued in prayer and encouragement.

One day, I was ministering to different sister and received a call from one of the missionaries at the church. She asked if I knew how to reach Betty. She went on to say that God would not allow her to pay her bills or do anything until she paid whatever Betty needed to have the eye surgery. I told her let me call Betty and that I would get back with her. When I reached Betty she began saying "I do not want to ask her for that much." She continued, "My husband had $1,000, however, I need more to have the rest of the procedure done." She felt that the remaining amount was too much to ask. I asked her if she recalled me reminding her of the scripture, "will thou be made whole?" I asked her if she remembered how much I had been fasting and praying with her. She then shared the amount. I asked if I could give the missionary her number so that they could make arrangements to receive the money. She agreed. On the way to taking her home from one of the services Betty stated, "When I can see again in this eye what do you want God to bless you with?" At that time, I simply asked if she would pray for my husband's salvation. She began immediately began praying immediately and asked that God would provide me with another vehicle—paid off!

Betty paid the fee for the surgery and went through the healing process. We went by to visit her and she was smiling and happy and was waiting to see what God was going to do in her healing process. The enemy continued to jab at her and we continued to pray. When Betty went back for her check-up her eyesight was returning and we were praising the Lord for hearing the cries of the righteous. After Betty was healed, she had forgotten her prayer requesting that the Lord bless me with a vehicle. God showed up and delivered a Volvo XC90 with leather seats, tv's, and my favorite color to my house on November 15, 2015. I immediately called her and shared that God had answered her prayer for me. We were both blessed! She could see and I had reliable transportation. To GOD be the glory!

Chapter 11
Hope for the Hopeless
By: Rosalind G.

I have been raising my grandchildren since my daughter passed in 2003. It has been tough. But God is stable no matter how rocky your journey might be.

At some point, I noticed that my water bill began to increase. Upon noticing it, I visited the City of Atlanta's Department of Water Company to complain about my inflated water bill. They said they would send someone out to check if there was a leak. However, they did not find one. My Landlord said he did not notice a leak either and that it would, therefore, be my responsibility to figure out the cause of the increased bill.

I continued to complain. The cycle of back-and-forth visits to the water company—coupled with technician visits to my house–went on for several years.

And then things came to a head.

I received a letter requesting that I go before a board for them to make a decision regarding who would be responsible for the outstanding bill. I explained the situation that my income had changed because of the death of my daughter and that there were only four people living in the home.

I also explained that over the last four to five years, I had major surgeries. And in addition to these issues, was this $10,000 water bill that increase for no logical reason. Nothing in my household had changed significantly for such a high increase in this bill to occur.

The board representative assumed that there had to be a leak. He told me that he could give me an adjustment if my landlord fixed the leak or running toilet. My landlord at the time would never do anything in a timely fashion. Therefore, time passed, with no repairs made.

To make matters worse, the board representative who was willing to assist, left the position after a year and a half. It looked hopeless that this issue would never be resolved.

Dread came over me. There were days I laid on my sick bed worrying about how I would get this matter resolved. I could not see a way out. I believed there was no help for me and my family. At some point, I would have to go in front of a judge and be accused of stealing water.

People knew my situation and they felt sorry for me and believed they were helping me by reconnecting my water. I was sick in bed for months at a time, I was going through surgery after surgery— four to be exact within a five-year time span. I was living off a fixed income, not knowing how to make ends meet. I would try to assist others in need and people would come and live at my house and never leave a dime for years while I was ill. Eventually, the water company took the meter. I had no water.

To make matters worse, my seven-year old granddaughter went to be with the Lord without warning! I was distraught.

But, I am a witness that Jesus is our Healer! Jesus is our Deliverer!

I kept believing the Word of God and began speaking HIs promises about healing over myself. I would watch ministry programs about healing prayers. I created "war walls" and posted scriptures from the Bible on them. I learned how to use my faith and to trust in the LORD my God.

This is when I met Sister Renay.

I was so weak and sick. Sister Renay was my warrior —my angel that the Lord sent to pray over me and my family daily and to encourage me. She called and came every day. I was so broken-hearted deep down in my soul. She was very kind and understanding.

One day I told her my story about that water bill that had me paralyzed with fear. I felt very helpless. I did not see a way out of this bondage. Sister Renay stood with me in prayer and started giving God praise for my breakthrough! She prayed that God would cut the bill in half. She believed that everything would work out in my favor. I was amazed at her faith, because I was so fragile, and she was so strong. She smiled, she praised God, she jumped, she was so very bold in her prayers and praise to God. She was so faithful in her walk and belief in His Word and promises.

When I went to court, I was so embarrassed. I took my bills and told them what happened to my grandbaby. They put me on a payment plan with my new bill. God knew I was sacrificing for others. I would get water from the neighbors and my daughter. My landlord never would come and fix the toilets. The City said it was not their fault. The landlord said it was not his fault. The city said they wanted all of the money owed to them—the full $10,000. They did care about my struggle.

But God cared.

God stepped in and the bill was cut in half! GOD performed a miracle almost immediately after we prayed. They worked a payment plan out and restored my water. I know God hears the cries of the righteous and answers them. I saw it for myself!

But there is more.

In 2021 God completely wiped out the debt owed for the water bill!!

The water company wrote to me and said they were giving me a fresh start and that I did not owe the remainder of the balance. Hallelujah!

Do you know what helped to protect my faith? My faith for healing. My faith for debt cancellation.

Renay's joy.

You see, Renay's mother died August 29, 2015. My granddaughter D. W. died September 3, 2015. While Renay was grieving, she was also nurturing. She never said a word. Her countenance never showed sadness or despair. She was always rejoicing and celebrating the Lord for her mother's long life and the opportunity of being her mother's daughter.

Renay "baby sat" me and "nursed" me back to health. It was God working through her to be my strength when I did not have enough strength to stand on my own.

I am forever grateful and thankful for her obedience and sacrifices. Mrs. Renay is a Woman of God, a Proverbs 31 Woman is who she is!

When you meet her and see her smile, you have met Jesus. I am grateful for my sister and friend in Christ.

Chapter 12
Can God Still Raise the Dead?
By: Sandra B.

My husband, the late Deacon Edmond O'Brien Burkhalter Sr., took very ill in February of 2012. I will never forget his words. He said, "Baby, my chest is hurting." I looked at him carefully and calmly. I pulled the truck around, helped him get in, and took him to Rockdale Hospital. They immediately took him to the back because he was having a heart attack. My Eldest son and his wife were in Afghanistan and the rest of my children were working. The doctors were giving me the bad news. I called my Bishop and his cousin, Sis. Izard and told them they were stabilizing my husband so that they could airlift him to Emory Midtown hospital. My heart was beating so fast. I said, "Oh Lord, help me— give me strength- this is a big one." I dropped in the chair crying, waiting on my ride to pick me up to take me to the second hospital.

Before leaving his room, I gave my husband kisses and my love like it was my last time seeing him alive.

This was very hard to handle. My husband asked, "Baby, am I going to die in the air?" I said, "Baby, you are going to be alright." I got to the hospital waiting for the airlift to land. My Church Family, Higher Calling Ministries (HCM) was there waiting for him with me. [I am so grateful for HCM. I would not have made it without my Bishop and First Lady Castilla, and the HCM family.]

My husband went into a coma. They revived him, but put him on life support to keep him alive. He was on twenty-two machines, but we never gave up!

Something rose up in me. I got radical faith, and called on the Bishop, elders, ministers, deacons, pastors, and my whole Church family to include Missionary Renay Allen. We prayed and prayed. "Mrs. Burkhalter, it's going to take a miracle for your husband," the doctors said. They told me he was dead. That they would not try to operate because he was gone. But the prayers of the saints rose to heaven.

Prayers rose from the East, West, North, and South. From across the seas in Afghanistan to the states in the US, people hooked their faith up with me. I could not move. All I could do was trust the Lord with all of my being. All I could say was, "I love You Lord." I asked the Lord to bring His manservant back like He did Lazarus. God said to fast for forty days—to sacrifice your flesh. I was faithful as his wife and did what God told me. God sent his Angel to operate on my husband from Texas. He did it! The doctor prayed with us and gave the procedure to God. God began to move. The doctors at

Emory asked, "What manner of man is this? It's the Lord's doing. Great is thy faithfulness" because my husband lived. My eldest Son and his wife had to return to Afghanistan. Before he departed, he said, "Lord, if you are real, please open my dad's eyes, show us a sign that he will live." God opened my husband's eyes. But, for a person who had been in a coma for a long period of time, his eyes were yellow.

The doctors said he would never walk, but God! Miracles took place. He performed a miracle not only on his heart, but his whole body.

God brought Deacon Burkhalter back whole. On October 23, 2024, Deacon Buckhalter passed on to glory but the Great Physician had shown us His power and how fasting and praying allowed us to witness a miracle of raising my husband from the dead. God did it. He is AMAZING!

Chapter 13
When God Knows Your Need
By: Sonja T.

In August 2016, my daughter was attending a back-to-school swim party at the YMCA Teen center. I was supposed to meet my former husband there so he could spend time with our daughter while she had fun with her friends. When I got there, he was sitting at the table with this really nice lady whose name was Renay Allen. She introduced herself to me and we started talking.

I could tell she was a woman of God.

My former husband left to go to the snack bar and Renay said that my husband was a really nice guy. I told her that we had been divorced since 2012. She started ministering to me about the love of God and she shared how the Lord had been faithful to her through her trials in her marriage. I sat at the table crying because I knew it was the Lord who sent her to share those words of wisdom.

She prayed for my ex-husband to get a job and for the Lord to continue to meet his needs.

Our interaction with Renay did not end at the pool because we exchanged numbers and Renay would send texts to check on the both of us. She would send words of encouragement to let me know we were in her heart.

Today, my ex-husband and I are very cordial with each other because of Renay. It was not always this way. When we first met, we were not getting along. Renay explained the importance of our daughter seeing us behave in a kind and cordial manner towards each other. Navigating the complexities of divorced parents is difficult. Adding a hostile relationship in front of our daughter breeds insecurities and unnecessary frustration during her most formative years.

I was thrown aback over Renay's kindness. I posted on my Facebook page the following statement, "I thought I was attending a back-to-school pool party, but the Lord sent a prayer warrior, whom I did not know, to minister to me. I was like the lady at the well with Jesus. I asked myself, "Who told her this stuff about me?" I know who told her.

It was God.

Chapter 14
God is Still Performing Miracles
By: Janet B.

My name is Janet B. and I'm a Diamond. My life is all about my God who has proven himself in so many ways. One way He has proven himself to me is in the below praise report.

I have a lifetime friend. To say that we have seen and done everything in this world is not an exaggeration. In 2013, I walked away from the street life of Macon, GA, in order to save my life when I say "walked away" I mean I left friends, acquaintances, and relatives.

After about six years, I established a new life. I reached out to a few friends (and I don't call many people friends), one of which was Gloria Griggs. While talking to her, I found out that she was in the fight of her life—she had stage four cancer. Despite this diagnosis, she was upbeat and faithful because we shared one very important point—our belief in God.

We began communicating about everything…every day. We shared common struggles and overcame similar obstacles. We didn't have secrets. I admired her for her strength and determination in her faith. I had seen this type of faith before.

I went through a similar experience with my mother and it didn't exactly turn out the way that I wanted, but the way God intended. Sometimes the pain was blinding, but I trusted my Father.

We were getting all great reports from Gloria's treatments. Everyone knew it was going to be okay. This went on for years until she went for some tests that we all hoped would end in the "bell ringing" ceremony. After she took the test, she was asked to come in for the results.

The test results were not good. After calling Gloria that evening. I heard something that I had not heard from her since her journey began—tears, yes, tears. Not tears of happiness, but of heartbreak. When I called she said, "Buckwheat, I can't believe this. You could not have told me that I was not getting better, cause I'm feeling better." I asked "what are you talking about? She answered that the nurse said that things were looking bad, and that she knew that her God didn't bring her through all of that for it to end in this manner. I told her that I was sorry to hear this news and that I would call Renay and get the prayer group going—which I did.

Well, Gloria wasn't satisfied. She made a call to the doctor and wanted him to go into more detail and explain what she was told the day before. He asked her to come in.

The doctor told her that she was misinformed about her reading the day before and that she only had a small spot left.

There were arrangements made to do radiation therapy on that spot.

Today, my friend, Gloria Griggs, is now cancer free! Praise the Lord!

Chapter 15
Nobody but God
By: Denise P.

It's amazing, on a daily basis I have the ability to reflect on the goodness of the Lord. My mind takes me back many years as a child. I briefly pondered over my existence. It's overwhelming! God chose me. Why? Well, He promised me He would be with me always, even until the end of time. Wow, in the Bible it is certain His Word is true! I've always believed God wouldn't leave me. I was taught as a child that in order to know God, I must develop a relationship with Him.

At an important turning point in my life, I had an eye-opening experience.

I was excited about my upcoming 50th birthday. I made several resolutions within my 49th year that were never achieved. Unexpectedly, four months before my birthday, I encountered a "bully". No, this was not your typical childhood bully, but a bully all the same.

I despise bullies! I teach my children to stand up to bullies. I help others who were bullied. Now, however, the ball was in my court. I experienced sore throat pain for many months. My visits to the doctor became frequent. I didn't claim any illness, but I wanted to assure myself that everything was fine. Thank God all of my visits were positive results. Five months had passed and my voice wasn't any better. I reflected back to 2007. That was the day I heard a voice whispering in my right ear while driving. The voice said, "You have cancer." It was so real! I immediately called my mother and explained my experience. I didn't know if God was trying to tell me something. Possibly the devil was trying to steal my joy. I prayed and moved forward. My life moved forward. I decided to go back to college. Two years later I graduated from college. I had a new job and a new outlook.

My spirit, however, was weighing on me. Even though professionals gave me rave reviews on my throat the Lord said, "Don't stop, move forward." Finally, I requested to see my ENT. My visit was successful! My doctor told me that he treats every patient as though he or she has cancer. I was impressed with his clarity. I thank God for sending me to a doctor who didn't take life for granted. I felt at ease. My tests were negative. However, he wasn't finished! Praise God! He wanted to be more thorough. He sent me for two more tests. Consequently, my results were yet again negative. His last request was a biopsy.

God spoke to me two days before my biopsy appointment and told me to go alone. Really? Lord, how can I tell my close-knit family that I was going alone when this was an out-patient procedure that requires assistance when going home?

Jesus worked it out.

I convinced my husband to work that particular day (he was out for a week to assist me after surgery). It worked! The day of my appointment my sister's plumbing created problems, therefore, she couldn't make it! Two down and two to go. My father had to work and my precious mother was on her way to meet me. I convinced her I would be finished by the time she arrived. I would meet her at home. She agreed, I knew it was nothing but God.

Two weeks later, I was sitting in his office waiting for the result. I wasn't worried because Isaiah 41:10 reminds me to "Fear not, for I am with you; be not dismayed, for I am your God; I will strengthen you, I will help you, I will uphold you with my righteous right hand."

By the time I arrived at my appointment my spirit was bubbling over! My doctor and I had a spirit filled conversation. We laughed and then I cried! My results were positive. I was diagnosed with larynx cancer. My tears lasted for approximately 1 minute. I told my doctor I was giving it to God.

He replied, "Well you're going to be just fine because you're a believer!" My thought pattern was to trust and believe. I knew God didn't bring me this far to leave me. I refused to allow any negativity to absorb my spirit. I was so overjoyed when I spoke to my family. I spoke healing. I praised God whenever I felt pain, anxiety, and joy! My spirit never wavered! I was unequivocally empowered! I faced that bully with the power and strength God gave me. I conquered it! God gave me life. Hallelujah, my pastor prayed for my faith, healing and strength. I spoke to my family individually! I spoke as though I had won the lottery. I kept my spirit at the level of excitement! Praise God, my family received the news with excellence.

Two weeks later, I was sitting in his office waiting for the result. I wasn't worried because Isaiah 41:10 reminds me to "Fear not, for I am with you; be not dismayed, for I am your God; I will strengthen you, I will help you, I will uphold you with my righteous right hand."

My sister Renay just happened to be traveling to my neck of the woods. She called out of the blue and my husband invited her to stop by. This was her first time ever visiting. We laughed and I shared with her the news the doctor had given me. She asked if she could anoint me and pray with me. She said God had sent her just for this purpose. We prayed and went outside to see the vehicle God had just blessed her with and we praised God all the more. She checked on me frequently waiting for the praise report, so we could praise God even more!

March came pretty quickly. I made it through! I reached 50 years of zest and zeal! Nothing but praise and glory! It's been three years since my diagnosis. On one cool night, I laid in my husband's arms talking nonstop like always. It dawned on me, God directed me to go to the doctor's appointment alone. He wanted to remind me that He is God and God alone!

GOD HEALED ME! IF HE DID IT FOR ME, HE CAN DO THE SAME FOR YOU!

Chapter 16

Prayer is a Sustainer

By: Verletta T.

Renay Allen is a wonderful Christian woman, wife, mother, and grandmother of whom I met in 1992. I've known her to always display Christian love, positivity, and encouragement to all whom she encounters. Never once has she spoken in a negative way about anyone. The way that she lives her life, and the characteristics that she displays are exemplary of a Christian.

She is also extremely active in church activities and belongs to several auxiliaries. She is a powerful prayer warrior, as well. When she prays, the power of God is felt. Anytime that my immediate and extended families have been in need of prayer, she is the one I call upon. Some examples of this have been when my mother became ill twelve years ago, until after her transitioning. Renay helped to make my mother's last days comfortable.

She was always happy. Both when praying and showing genuine concern during conversations.

God knows I wanted to be with my mother and I shared with Renay that I needed to get there as the doctor's had given my mother news that was very disheartening. Renay is a confidante. She prayed and God showed favor. I was able to spend time with my mother during her last years on earth until she went to be with the Lord. My mother's life was extended and I know God did it for me. She has also prayed for my sons during illnesses and other challenging times.

Prior to, during, and after having twenty-nine surgeries over a time frame of eight years, Renay has never stopped praying for and with me.

She is a Virtuous Woman (Proverbs 31). She is faithful and loving to her husband (Proverbs 31:11-12), and actively involved in her children's and grandchild's well-being (Proverbs 31:27-28).

I am so grateful that the Lord has placed a prayer warrior in my life. She leads by example, and passionately inspires people to look beyond whatever unforeseen circumstances or issues that they may be facing. From her Christ-like example, which is led by the Holy Spirit, she gives all praise and worship to God.

I said all of this to note how important it is to have prayer warriors in your life. Prayer is a sustainer!

Chapter 17
I had to Take this Time to Give this Testimony
By: Leatha E.

I dealt with a whole lot of turmoil because the enemy did not want me to win the victory through Christ Jesus. I do not recall the exact date that I called Renay to intercede for me and my family as I prayed with her on several occasions for many situations that I was facing. I am so grateful she had the willingness to put us first.

My sons were facing several charges with Cobb County as they were out on bond for gun and drug charges. They were racially profiled and were illegally stopped. The cops threw my children down on the freezing ground with no coats on a very cold winter day. The District Attorney offered a bargain that they would serve three months at the diversion center, produce clear drug tests, and afterwards, all charges would be dismissed with no felony history or jail time.

On another occasion, when I was in a car accident, my attorney got an offer for one of my lawsuits. I was facing eviction because I was unable to pay rent. Through prayer and believing God, all of my back rent was paid and I was moved into a new place with four to six months' rent paid.

JESUS!!! GLORY!!! I won the case against the insurance company. They tried to make me pay 20% for a not-at-fault accident. God saw this injustice. They, however, had to pay me as their insurer! We went to arbitration, I won, and they had to return my deductible.

God is so amazing.

Remember, it is important to have a prayer warrior who can touch and agree with you when going through fiery trials. God heard our cries and answered!

Chapter 18
God Heals Little Children
By: Renay Allen

When my daughter, Kristine, was in second grade, she would wet her clothing, so I would have to send her an extra set of clothes. We could not understand why she would wet herself while awake. I decided to take her to see a Urologist. They gave her medications, a regiment to use the restroom every two hours and asked that we come back for follow-ups. This did not change her circumstance after having several visits. They decided to do a stress test on her and found she had incontinence. The moment any liquid entered her bladder it would immediately protrude out and she could not hold her urine.

Upon seeing the doctor, he shared that he could place stents in her as the first option. I would not allow that to happen to her at such a young age. The doctor also suggested Botox. I would not allow that option either. We left the doctor's office not agreeing with any of the suggested remedies.

As we walked to the elevator, I explained that the doctors could not heal her, but that our Father in Heaven is the Healer. I asked her if we could pray together as soon as we got to the car. She said, "Okay mommy." I clearly remember holding her little hand and asking God to touch her and to heal her bladder so that she could hold her urine until she was able to get to the restroom.

We prayed and believed together for her healing.

I can assure you that she no longer suffers with incontinence and she is now 17 years of age. God healed her when the doctors could not help her.

What a MIGHTY GOD we serve!

Chapter 19
God Can Restore
By: Renay Allen

On July 26, 2023, I received a frantic call from my daughter, K, who was crying and requesting that I please pick her up from school. I was concerned as this was her first day back to school. When I arrived, she was waiting at the door for me to pick her up. I was not sure what had happened. She just sobbed all the way home. I would occasionally ask her if she was okay. K came home, took a shower but did not get up for school the next day. When I entered her room, she did not respond. I left to take my son to school and returned home, however, there was still no movement from her. I asked my son if he had any idea what happened to his sister. He said, "no." After getting off work. I began trying to reach out to her. She never moved, only tears poured from her eyes. She was catatonic. I asked her again in a couple of hours what had happened to her. I began praying and telling the enemy he could not have her.

The following day, I called the school to find answers as to what happened to her. I asked them to roll the cameras. I was desperate. It was like a scene out of a movie. K never moved, ate, or responded in any way. I called the school counselor to see if an investigation had taken place and called her friends to see if they had any insight. I then asked one of my older daughters to come over to see if she could get her up. There was no success.

By this time, I was totally distraught as to why this behavior continued. I did not know what to do, but I kept crying and praying for her to snap out of what I now know was depression. The counselor had given me specific information on who to call if this behavior continued. I called one of the nurses at the church to ask her if she had encountered anything like this? She said she had not but that she would connect me with a sister that went through a bout of depression similar to what I described. She sent me her contact information and I found out her sister worked with mental health. We began praying and she told me to turn on the lights, clap my hands and keep praying. She explained that the longer she stays in this state the longer it will take her to get out of it. At midday— Day 4— I asked my other daughter to get off work and to come over. I explained I would have to have K removed from the house, as the spirit of depression could not dwell there. I gave God full authority to eradicate it from my house and I wanted my child to live. I made a call and a group of counselors were dispatched to my home to try and speak with her but there was still no activity, except for breathing. I asked my daughter to help me get K cleaned up as I was going to request they take her to the Children's Psych ward. At this facility, she was walking around with her eyes closed when I would make her get up to take a shower or go to the restroom. This was a notable change from her behavior at home. This spirit was determined to take her out. I was determined she was going to live! All while this was taking place, the prayer team and I did not let up. I would go to the hospital every day to try and get her to eat, talk or respond. After about the fifth day in the hospital, God had me take my granddaughter and great niece to the hospital to try and get K to return to normal. They got in the bed with her, they danced and acted like they were making tic toc videos. The doctors would come in frequently throughout the day to see if she was coming around.

The day the girls came, they determined that this must stop! We prayed and they were able to get her to smile, laugh, take a few sips of water. By the end of the day, they had her talking and smiling. The doctors were able to stop the medicines. She begged them to please allow her to go home. They released her the following day.

My daughter has never spoken of what happened to her, but she did return to school after speaking with the counseling team and expressed what she did not want them to do. Her teachers, staff, family, and friends were all calling to check on her.

The girls from school shared with me that K has started a Bible Study with them and they believed that because she was making such an impact the enemy attacked her.

To all parents: Please— no matter what—if your child strays, please do not give up on them. Call on the saints to pray. In the morning's, during K's time at the facility, I would have the family member who was sitting with my child to put me on speaker in the mornings while dropping my son off to school while I prayed and worshiped. The staff at the hospital would stay until I arrived to tell me how my prayers were moving them. They would ask me to call and pray with them. They wanted to know where my church was. Prayer makes a huge impact. For, some things happen only with fasting and praying. If she did not eat or drink, neither did I for about 10 days.

She is Alive! She's back!!!

Chapter 20
If He Did It for Her, He Will Do It for Me
By: Renay Allen

I shared in an earlier Chapter a testimony from a sister whose water bill was $10,000. The same thing happened to me and I was clueless as to what was going on. I just kept receiving water bills upwards of $400, $600, and then $1,000 until the bill was $6,000. I was on the phone with the water company disputing all of these bills as we had not significantly changed the amount of water we were using in my household.

I had a plumber come out and fix a pipe to ensure there were no leaks, however, the next bill that came out was even higher. I called the Landlord and explained that there was a leak somewhere and he asked me to send him a copy of my bill. The water company confirmed that the leak was not on their end. I was adamant that I could not afford to pay the bill.

As time passed, I was out mowing the lawn and noticed a cluster of flying bugs in a certain area of the yard. I consistently kept the bushes and hedges cut as well sprayed my lawn to keep the weeds down. I had never seen a swarm of bugs in an area of my yard like that before. I inspected and noticed that the yard was wet in a particular area. I called the Landlord and stated that I believe I found the leak and located a busted pipe. I asked him to have a plumber to come out and look. One plumber came out and confirmed this to be the case. His price to replace the pipes and dig up the yard was very expensive. The Landlord called out another company that was more reasonable. We had to wait for the gas company to come out and put flags where the gas lines were located. By this time, my water bill had reached over $6,000.00. I begin to pray all the more. I submitted the receipts to the water company expecting to have a credit and they stated that I still had a balance of almost $2,000.00. I continued to pay what I could.

My next-door neighbor was moving and I went to wish her and her family well. She and her parents was upset that the original buyer for her home had reneged on the contract, especially given that she had bought another home about 4 hours away. We prayed that God would show her favor and send her another buyer soon for the same amount or more than she was originally asking. I shared with her about the pipes and she said that this also happened to her months back. She stated those pipes were found to be faulty.

The city was offering help for the water bill for renters and I called to make an appointment. There was a 6-months wait before the resources opened up. When I finally got an appointment and went in, the lady heard my story. She asked me to submit receipts from the repairs. She assured me the water company would pay 3 months of the back balance in about 6 - 8 weeks, but to keep paying what I could.

I jumped up and began praising God in the office, Tears of joy were streaming from my eyes. When the company finally paid, I received a credit of $3500 after the past due balance was paid. Who wouldn't serve a GOD like that! He is so worthy of all the praise.

By the way… God sent my neighbor a buyer within 60 days and she was able to close and have piece-of-mind. She and her parents have thanked me multiple time for praying with them on the matter.

Chapter 21
When You Receive Bad News Unexpectedly
By: Renay Allen

On February 2, 2023, I went to the doctor and received the worst report that I can remember. The doctors stated that my left ventricle was slightly enlarged, referred me to a cardiologist, and scheduled me for an echocardiogram. They stated that my heartbeat was lower than normal, there was swelling in my legs, and I was referred to the vein doctor. In addition, the doctors saw something on my left breast, so I had a follow up mammogram and sonogram. My blood pressure was also out of control.

But, I trusted God and His report. I rebuked this report of the enemy and anything else surrounding this issue and casted it back to hell. I instantly began praying and solicited the prayers from others. [Note: I will continue to share the praise report as it unfolds…]

I received a message that all kinds of prayers were being lifted up for me. My charge from these prayer warriors was that I remain steadfast and unmovable and that I would abound in faith. That I should belief in the Word and the report of the Lord!! To standing in faith and believe that by His stripes, I am healed. Others were sending messages stating they were looking forward to the praise report. I could not wait to send over the following praise report.

The first praise report…

On, 2/10/2023, I shared, I am leaving the ER and my heart looks healthy, my blood pressure has come down to normal levels. My blood work and EKG all look fine. Thank you Jesus!

The praise report continues…
My praise report is still unfolding in segments.
On the morning of March 11, 2023, I went back to have a mammogram and sonogram for my left breast. I had a set of images done and then they called me back again for another set. I was then called back to see the doctor. ALL IS WELL! I did not have to have the sonogram. I learned I had dense mass in my breast.

Further praise report blessings….

I saw the cardiologists on 3/17/23 and the doctor on 3/30/23. I continued to share the good news. It's His report I will believe! Hallelujah!! But, you know that when it rains it pours. Another issue arose. My vehicle registration was due to expire on 2/28/23. I spoke with a sister from another church and she called a mechanic. I took the vehicle to the mechanic Sunday night and picked it up Monday after work on 2/27/23. I had to drive the vehicle 100 miles before I could take it to the emission place. The good thing is that the location was in Powder Springs, GA, so the ride home gave me good mileage to measure on the return. By 5:50pm I had driven about 99 miles. I arrived at the emission place right at closing and they took me. It passed, Hallelujah! I, then, drove to Kroger and used the Kiosk to purchase the decal. What an on-time God HE is!! Another sister from HCM gave funds to assist me with getting my daughter's laptop repaired. My daughter's laptop died and since she is an IT major and needs her laptop for programming class, this was truly a blessing. She received other monetary donations which allowed her to get her laptop repaired so that her school work would not be interrupted. Praise the Lord!

It continues...

I went to Emory hospital on 3/17/2023. The grand finale to my testimony is that the cardiologist stated that ALL is well with my heart!

Because of the good condition of my heart, he stated that he did not understand why I was there to see him in the first place!

MY GOD IS SO GOOD!

Chapter 22
God is Dependable
By: Kraynewskia O.

As a woman when you find out you're pregnant you pray for a full-term safe delivery, You do everything in your power to not stress especially, when your husband is at sea preparing for deployment and your closest family is 9 hours away.

On the morning of March 9th, I was working from home. I stood up to warm my tea and I felt a large amount of water run down my leg. Almost immediately, I knew my water had broken at 24 weeks and 3 days gestation. I took the time to text my siblings then my mom. While working remotely, I told my team that I had a medical emergency and needed someone to run the meeting I was leading. At the time, my supervisor was out on maternity leave and I was the only other social worker on my team that had been in my role for over 6 months and I could not imagine how my team would manage.

My mom called and said that I needed to go to the hospital right away and encouraged me to call the ambulance. She immediately began to pray for me and the baby. I had just moved to a new state and hadn't familiarized myself with anything but the local grocery store and church. I looked up the closest emergency room and drove myself, since it was a 13 minute drive. When I got there they told me they were a free standing hospital so they would have to transport me to another hospital about 15 minutes away where there were OB/GYNs that could assist. I immediately panicked because I thought that I had just avoided an ambulance ride. While I was not having any pain, I remember this being the most humbling experience ever. I had several nurses helping me undress and while there were about 8 to 9 medical staff in the room all doing different things, I still had to allow them to check me to ensure they did not see any signs of the baby coming. Once things settled down I spoke to someone in accounting and they let me know that my insurance was not valid. I was flabbergasted because each month my job takes the money out of my check so I did not understand. That just added to the things that I needed to follow up on.

Once the ambulance came and took me to the hospital, they let me know that I would be staying until I delivered. That meant I could be in the hospital for more than 10 weeks. I immediately prayed to God because that was too long. Being a geriatric social worker, I started to feel the pain of my clients when they were in the hospital for long periods of time. I had to just sit in bed most of the day. I was unable to put on pants, go outside, or shower by myself. However, at the time the worst part was receiving the medication to keep the baby in place. That made me feel like I had the flu.

I can say God was truly with me. During this time I did my best to focus on letting God handle things. Day and night I would listen to gospel to remain calm. Over and over I would hear that God was a dependable God! I would imagine leaving all my problems in his hands. As I did, my husband was able to make it to the hospital before my daughter was born and I was able to have a church member I had just met less than a month ago, by my side every day for several hours until my husband came back from sea. Until this day I still believe she is an Angel sent just for my family.

After making it four days with no labor activity I was taken down to get an ultrasound. The doctor had a really hard time taking pictures due to the fluid being so low. They let me know that I would be going down to labor and delivery. I spoke to the doctor and he let me know that African American kids born before term have the highest survival rate out of the other races. I sat there 5 hours with no labor activity so they sent me back to the antepartum unit.

As I recall, it was about 4 or 5 centimeters and I was having contractions in my back. When the doctor came in to check she let me know that my child was coming tail first. They immediately rushed me down to complete an emergency c-section. I was afraid but I immediately called my husband then my mom to let them know.

It would be an understatement to say "God was Good", it was Amazing! At 25 weeks gestational age my child was born. The children's hospital was right next to the general hospital and they took great care of delivering her safely. She remained in the NICU for 104 days and while there she did not have to have one surgery. God is Amazing.

She's now 2 years old and developing more and more. She continues to be as determined and feisty as the day she came out. God is dependable. This would not have been possible without the prayers of the righteous.

Chapter 23
Only By Faith
By: India A.

Back in 2010, I was given the opportunity to attend my high school senior trip to China. I instantly thought to myself, "I cannot afford $5,000, and neither can my parents." I was wishful for a moment because the trip was relevant to the courses that I was taking at the time. It would be my first time out of the country and my second time flying. How cool would that be!

After receiving the flier of the trip, I must have stuck it in my bag, but never showed it to my mom. It must have been God, because my mom came to a PTA meeting and found out about the opportunity. After this discovery she instantly asked me, "India, how could you not tell me about the opportunity to go to China?" I informed her that I knew we could not afford it. My mom had lost her job back in the 2008 recession and had not worked since. We were in the process of losing the only home I had known. It was the home my grandmother had owned for more than 30 years. We lived there because we lost the home my mom had just built in 2005. We were tight on finances and it was evident because there were times where we went without certain utilities.

My mom had seven kids. I was selling snacks at school to help with family finances. The money I received from selling snacks also helped me purchase personal things that I needed to pay for senior prom and activity days.

Failing to believe that God would provide the finances for this trip were doubts the devil had planted in my head.

After hearing my skepticisms, my mom asked, "Do you not know who you belong to? Do you not know that if you ask God, that he will provide. Have you prayed about this?" She instantly stated, "We MUST Pray now!" We did. When she finished, she instantly began to counteract all my doubts. She reminded me of who I am in Christ and the community of faith that I have around me. At the time, I was in the top 3% of my class, president of the Jobs for Georgia Graduates, Treasurer of the 12th Grade SGA, a Cadette in Girl Scouts, the President of the Young Adult Ministries at Beulah Cathedral COCHUSA, and an active young adult in my community. My mom instantly encouraged me to reach out to my community and tell them that I had a chance to spend 10 days in China and visit three cities.

I began to tell my mentors, the staff and program coordinators of programs of which I participated. I had conversations with my peers, high school support groups, church members and former boss from working at the local farmer's market. With that, blessings began to flow like crazy. The word began to spread like wildfire. The East Atlanta Village farmers market and community got together and collected donations for me. The East Atlanta Kids Club spotlighted me and helped me conduct a raffle fundraiser. I raised money with my classmates at school via fundraisers. Extended family and church members began to mail me checks. By the time all the funds were due, I had enough money to purchase the trip, passport and even had extra money for spending.

Like, look at God! He had exceeded my Goal!

From the moment I understood that I should NEVER doubt God, but seek Him for things that I need, and to pray without ceasing, I realized that I must share this testimony with the world.

[I can remember my mother doing this same thing with my older sister for her to go on a missionary trip to Africa with church. God is so faithful!]

I was blessed to be able to send out thank you letters, have a showcase of my experience, and tell my testimony to those around me. During this journey, I learned so much and was able to relate to the verses that my mom would have me to read and discuss in church. The top five verses are:

Proverbs 3:5–6
Trust in the LORD with all your heart, and do not lean on your own understanding. In all your ways acknowledge Him, and He will make straight your paths.

Joshua 1:9
"Have I not commanded you? Be strong and courageous. Do not be frightened, and do not be dismayed, for the LORD your God is with you wherever you go."

Philippians 4:6–7 (NIV)
Do not be anxious about anything, but in every situation, by prayer and petition, with thanksgiving, present your requests to God. And the peace of God, which transcends all understanding, will guard your hearts and your minds in Christ Jesus.

Isaiah 41:13
"For I, the LORD your God, hold your right hand; it is I who say to you, 'Fear not, I am the one who helps you.'"

1 Peter 5:6–7
Humble yourselves, therefore, under the mighty hand of God so that at the proper time He may exalt you, casting all your anxieties on Him, because He cares for you.

I will never forget these verses. Until this very day, he still reminds me that he is my one and only True Provider.

Chapter 24
Wait on the LORD
By: Rita J.

Hi my name is Rita. J. I moved to Atlanta, Georgia in March of 2018. Although it was a journey, I wanted to move to be closer to my older children, who have been living in Atlanta for many years. I did not want to move and have to live off of my children, therefore, I was looking for a job before I got here.

My husband had moved to Atlanta before I did. He did live with one of our daughters for a period of time and thought he had a job, but it did not work out. We, however, did not give up. I decided to keep looking for a job. I traveled to Atlanta twice on two interviews and during one of them, I was certain I had secured a position. Again, disappointment–no position. I was heartbroken.

I decided to attend the church, Higher Calling, that my husband was attending while he was in Atlanta. When I attended, the worship was so real. The people were so real. I really enjoyed the worship experience. During that time, I went up to the altar for prayer and Sister Renay Allen came up and prayed for me. Anytime I would go up for prayer she would pray for me. I found out she was also praying for my husband. She even asked one time, "do you mind if I would pray for you?" I told her, "No." For who would turn down prayer?

No position had still come my way, so I went back home to Jackson, MS, and I prayed. I was on my knees and I felt the Lord did not want me and my husband separated—me in Mississippi and he in Georgia. Although we had my husband's social security as financial support, it was not enough for both of us to live on. So he took a position with a real estate firm.

All of a sudden, one day I was sitting at my desk in Jackson and I received a phone call from a company in Sandy Springs, GA and the lady wanted to perform a phone interview with me of which I agreed. She, then, phoned me back and asked me to come in for a personal interview. I went as soon as I could, which was a week later. While I was there, they suddenly called me back for another interview on that Friday and again for another face-to-face interview on that Saturday where I met two of the partners.

Praise God, that Sunday before I left town, I received an email from that company and they offered me the position. I know that it was GOD answering my prayer. I know that it was God because I was turned down twice, but GOD had something better for me.

Not only did this company offer me the job, but they also offered me the pay that I wanted and the paid time off (PTO) I desired. I thank GOD for this job. Driving in Georgia's traffic concerned me, but GOD worked that out as well. I catch an express bus every day. I do not have to drive and I appreciate that, as I live in Lawrenceville, GA which is a good distance from my job, but it is close to where my children live. Thank you, Sis.

Renay, for being persistent in prayer for me and my family. Please continue to do so. Thank you Jesus!

LIST OF CONTRIBUTORS

Renay Allen

India Allen

Janet Billingslea

Tony Brown

Sandra Burkhalter

Socrates Ellis

Cherry English

Leatha Edwards

Rosalind Grooms

Arthur Johnson

Rita Jordan

Kraynewskia Onibode

Denise Person

Sonja Turner

George Terrell

Deitre Terrell

Verletta Thompson

www.ingramcontent.com/pod-product-compliance
Lightning Source LLC
LaVergne TN
LVHW051658080426
835511LV00017B/2624